OCT 08 2015

From Empty Lot to Building

Meg Greve

rourkeeducationalmedia.com

Teaching Focus:
Concepts of Print- Have students find capital letters and punctuation in a sentence. Ask students to explain the purpose for using them in a sentence.

Before Reading:

Building Academic Vocabulary and Background Knowledge

Before reading a book, it is important to set the stage for your child or students by using pre-reading strategies. This will help them develop their vocabulary, increase their reading comprehension, and make connections across the curriculum.

1. *Read the title and look at the cover. Let's make predictions about what this book will be about.*
2. *Take a picture walk by talking about the pictures/photographs in the book. Implant the vocabulary as you take the picture walk. Be sure to talk about the text features such as headings, Table of Contents, glossary, bolded words, captions, charts/diagrams, or Index.*
3. Have students read the first page of text with you then have students read the remaining text.
4. *Strategy Talk – use to assist students while reading.*
   - *Get your mouth ready*
   - *Look at the picture*
   - *Think…does it make sense*
   - *Think…does it look right*
   - *Think…does it sound right*
   - *Chunk it – by looking for a part you know*
5. *Read it again.*
6. *After reading the book complete the activities below.*

Content Area Vocabulary
Use glossary words in a sentence.

architect
community
construction crew
foundation
level
lot

After Reading:

Comprehension and Extension Activity

After reading the book, work on the following questions with your child or students in order to check their level of reading comprehension and content mastery.

1. *Why is teamwork between the architect and construction crew important?* (Asking Questions)
2. *Explain why the foundation of a building is important.* (Summarize)
3. *Should the flowers and plants be planted before, during, or after the construction of the building? Why?* (Inferring)
4. *Do you know someone who has one of the jobs from the book? What job do they have? Share with us.* (Text to self connection)

Extension Activity

Think about it! Look around your home or school and notice all the things needed to make up the building. Are there flowers in front of your school? Who put them there? Are there light switches in your home? Who put them there? Think about the different jobs needed and choose one to explain to your classmates or parents. Draw a picture of the person you chose and label their equipment or tools. Next, present to your parents or classmates on what they do and how this job is reflected in your house or school.

An empty **lot** sits on the corner. What can it be? A park, a school, a store? The **community** needs a store, and a business owner wants to build one right here.

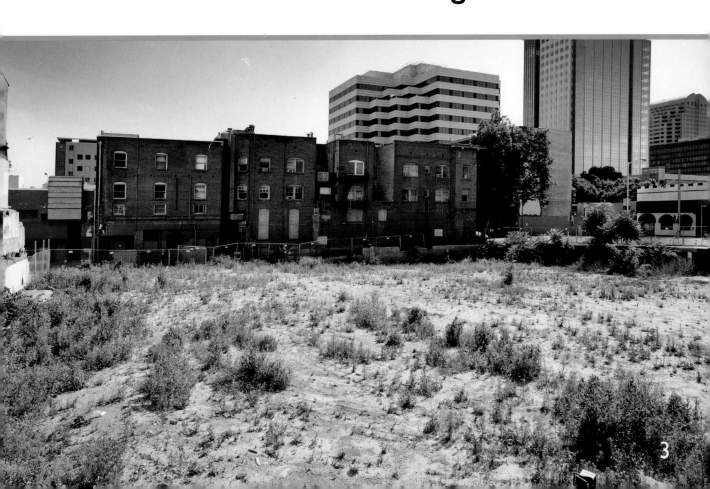

What is it like to build a building, and who builds it? There is a lot of work to do. Let's get started.

Job Shop

Business owners have to ask the city permission to build a store on an empty lot. This could take a long time and cost lots of money!

The owner hires an **architect** to draw the plans needed to build the store.

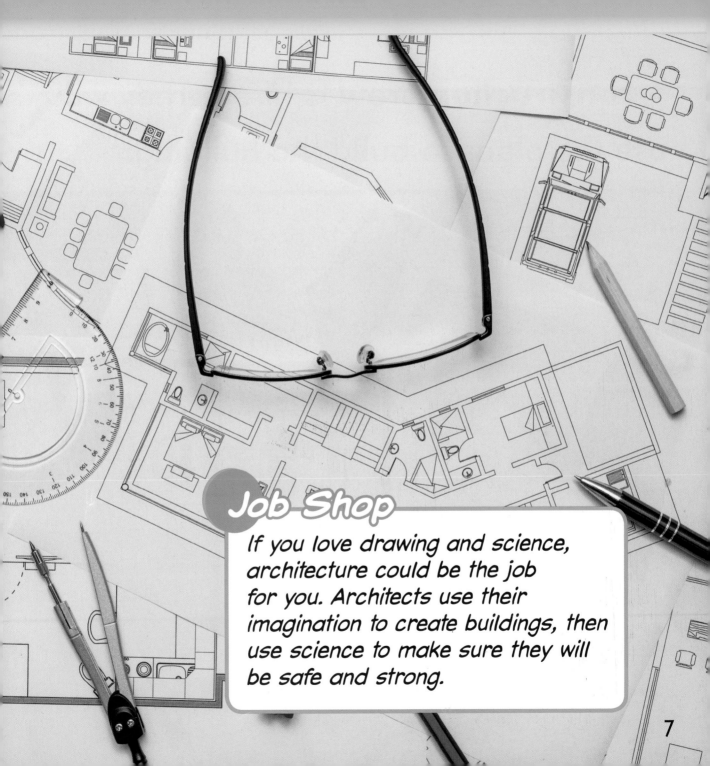

Job Shop

If you love drawing and science, architecture could be the job for you. Architects use their imagination to create buildings, then use science to make sure they will be safe and strong.

A **construction crew** is hired. They will use the plans to build the building.

Job Shop

A blueprint is the picture and information about the building. The special paper used is either blue with white drawings or white with blue drawings.

Many people work on a construction crew. Every person has a special skill needed to build a building.

Who Is On This Crew?

large
machine
operator

carpenter

mason

laborer

electrician

plumber

pipefitter

roofer

First the ground is made **level**. It also has to be strong enough to support the building. If the ground is not level or strong enough, the building could end up crooked!

Job Shop

The Leaning Tower of Pisa in Italy is a perfect example of the ground not being strong enough. It leans due to poor planning and soft ground!

Once the ground is flat, the **foundation** is poured. Most foundations are made of cement.

Job Shop

A cement mason must have just the right mix of cement so when it hardens, the foundation does not crack.

Job Shop

Cement is made up of limestone, clay, aluminum, and iron. It is made into a powder and then mixed with sand, gravel, and water.

After the foundation is dry, the framers build the frame of the building. Just like us, a building has a skeleton to help hold it up.

Job Shop

A framer uses strong materials, such as wood and steel, to create the walls, floors, and ceilings of a building.

17

A contractor and crew will put in walls, windows, and doors. Now the building is starting to look like the plans the architect drew.

Job Shop

Contractors oversee all of the workers on a job site.

Electricians and plumbers install lighting, sinks, and bathrooms. The roofers finish the roof.

Job Shop

Electricians and plumbers are skilled workers who must have a certain amount of education to perform these jobs.

19

Landscape architects design the outside of the building. They plant flowers, trees, and gardens, design walkways, and might even install a bike rack.

Finally! The store is open and ready for business!

Photo Glossary

architect (AR-ki-tekt): Someone who designs buildings and gives plans on how to build them.

community (kuh-MYOO-nuh-tee): A group of people who live and work near one another.

construction crew (kuhn-STRUHKT-shuhn KROO): A group of people who work together to build something.

 **foundation** (foun-DAY-shuhn): The base on which a building is built.

 **level** (LEV-uhl): A surface that is flat and even.

 **lot** (LOT): A piece of land that is empty.

Index

Websites to Visit

www.sciencekids.co.nz/sciencefacts/engineering/buildings.html

wonderopolis.org/wonder/what-does-an-architect-do

www.softschools.com/facts/wonders_of_the_world/leaning_tower_of_pisa_
facts/93

About the Author

Meg Greve lives in Chicago with her husband Tom, and her two children, Madison and William. They live on a street where lots of construction workers are working together to build bigger and better houses.

Meet The Author!
www.meetREMauthors.com

www.rourkeeducationalmedia.com

PHOTO CREDITS: Cover © David Jones, Joel_420; title page © Katarzyna Mazurowska; page 3 © Slobo Mitic; page 4 © Kasia Bialasiewicz; page 5 © GlobalStock; page 6 © Yuri Arcurs; page 7 © Jelena83; page 8 © Stevica Mrdja; page 9 © 28fortescue; page 10 © kozmoat98; page 11 © Moodboard, Nagy-Bagoly Arpad, Dmitry Kalinovsky, auremar, Highway Starz; page 12 © Katarzyna Mazurowska, page 13 Katarzyna Mazurowska Worapat Maitriwong; page 14 © Redshed; page 15 © Ulrich Mueller; page 16 © Vicki Reid; page 17 © Jeffrey B. Banke; page 18 © photographerlondon; page 19 ©auremar; page 20 © WoodenDinosaur; page 21 © Albert Pego

Edited by: Luana Mitten
Cover and Interior design by: Jen Thomas

Library of Congress PCN Data

From Empty Lot to Building/Meg Greve
(Little World Communities and Commerce)
ISBN (hard cover)(alk. paper) 978-1-63430-059-9
ISBN (soft cover) 978-1-63430-089-6
ISBN (e-Book) 978-1-63430-116-9
Library of Congress Control Number: 2014953338

Printed in the United States of America, North Mankato, Minnesota

Also Available as:

ROURKE'S
e-Books